Did You Hear Him Calling?
Did You Hear Jesus Calling?

Did You Hear Him Calling?
Did You Hear Jesus Calling?

ShTruth Poetry

DID YOU HEAR HIM CALLING?
DID YOU HEAR JESUS CALLING?

iUniverse books may be ordered through booksellers or by contacting:

iUniverse
1663 Liberty Drive
Bloomington, IN 47403
www.iuniverse.com
844-349-9409

Because of the dynamic nature of the Internet, any web addresses or links contained in this book may have changed since publication and may no longer be valid. The views expressed in this work are solely those of the author and do not necessarily reflect the views of the publisher, and the publisher hereby disclaims any responsibility for them.

Any people depicted in stock imagery provided by Getty Images are models, and such images are being used for illustrative purposes only.
Certain stock imagery © Getty Images.

ISBN: 978-1-4917-5234-0 (sc)
ISBN: 978-1-4917-5235-7 (e)

Print information available on the last page.

iUniverse rev. date: 01/10/2024

When I was making the choice to write this book, I opened the bible to these scriptures. (KJV)

The Lord answer, me and said. Write the vision; make it plain upon the tables, that he may run that readeth it. For the vision is yet for an appointed time, but at the end it shall speak and not lie; though it tarry, wait for it; because it will surely come, it will not tarry. Behold, his soul which is lifted up is not upright in him; but the just shall live by his faith. Habakkuk 2:3

Another scripture said open the book and write. It will be sweet as a honey comb, and bitter to thy belly. Ezekiel 3:3

When Jesus showed John the vision he was making way to come to be an example to his people.

I now accept that God used me as an example to make way to come into my life.

What then shall we say to these things? If God is for us, who can be against us? Romans 8:31

I remember when there came about a sudden peace.

I was lying in the hospital bed and a hymn came to me.

I could feel the people praying, all I could sing in my head was.

Couldn't hear nobody pray.

Couldn't hear nobody pray.

Way down yonder by myself.

Couldn't hear nobody pray.

And the spirit of Jesus brought the anointing, and a lot of my body felt better. I did not think the same anymore. And I made the vow to go all the way with the Lord. I repeatedly said. When I get home, I'm cutting off all my friends.

I'm going to get on my knees at church and call on Jesus until I be endued with power from on high. I made up my mind that I decided to make Jesus my choice.

Some Scriptures are from the King James Bible

I will never leave you nor forsake you.
In my Father's house are many mansions, if
it were not so, I would have told you.
If God be for you, it's greater, then the world against you.
Behold I will send a comforter, which is the Holy Ghost.
Seek me while I am near.
Many shall seek and not enter in.
Who do you say that I am?
John 14:2

John 14:18–28

Psalms 121

I will lift my eyes to the hill from which cometh my help.
My help cometh from the Lord.
The Lord who made heaven and earth.

He will not suffer thy foot to be moved.
He that keepeth thee, will neither slumber nor sleep

The Lord is thy keeper the Lord is thy shade

The sun shall not smite thee by day nor the moon by night.
He shall preserve they soul, and even forever more

I would like to thank God Jesus Christ my Lord and Savior for being the head of my life. I thank my father for being tolerant, to my mother R.I.P I told you someday I would be on T.V, I would like to thank my family for being there and friends who were unconditional. I thank my Pastor for helping me to become productive, to her mother R.I.P I will always remember the vacations together. I would like to thank my friends that had a role in my life but in time we grew apart. I would like to thank all the specialist, doctors, and team at Saint Peters University Hospital for taking care of me. I thank my Church members for your prayers. Through it all I over came by God's grace and mercy.

It's toward the end of the school year and Neosha's getting ready to graduate. Deep within herself, she doesn't know where this is going to take her, everybody she called her friends are now given her their backend and she is shattered with speechless ends. She has done a lot of research on career choices and she has chosen one that she desired to learn more about. So she approaches her teacher about it and she said immediately.

'oh no you can't do this! It will be too hard for you.

Neosha looked in dismay. Well I feel I can do this I'm the kind of person to when I put my heart on something I want to do it get will get done.

Yeah but I feel you should want to do something else.

Her teachers don't think much on her because they had another agenda.

Look Neosha! Why don't you stay back another year so that we can teach you how to do this?

No! I hate this school it seems like every time I try to become something there is always someone telling me what I can and can't do. I hate that. Then all of a sudden people tried to persuade her the best way they could, but she had her mind made up. Neosha felt the school itself was a set back because she rather had gone to the high school in her district. Where they taught advanced things, and where there was more opportunity. Neosha felt she worked to reach this point so she was going to start chasing opportunities, by making college her focal point.

Graduation day she walked across the stage with a smirk on her face saying internally. This is not it there is more to life than what I see. Later what people think, later to hear what they say, I can truly say I don't care. As I began to acknowledge the power of God I knew he would help me I plan to learn more of you. I am going to start a new beginning.

Neosha came home and her brother's girlfriend that was over.

Hey flaw I want to go to college; I refuse to stick around here and be nothing. Bob Marley said "in this great future, you can't forget your past, so dry your tears I say." My teachers made me feel like I will be nothing, I always wanted more but I was limited.

Yeah Sapphire I agree with you, if you feel you want to start college then go ahead. Flaw replied.

Look I believe you can do it. Right now I'm studying law follow your heart.

While in the midst of preparing for College, before she reached the point of completing applications, she had gone to one orientation being the youngest one in the circle. The instructor asked each one why they chose to go to college, what is the major you are applying for? And if you don't mind saying your age, how old are you? Each one went around saying what their purpose was and so it was Neosha's turn.

Hi my name is Neosha, but my nickname is Sapphire. My potential major is Radiography. The reason why I chose Middle because it is local and I feel this will be a great opportunity that will help me in my future my objective is to find a good paying job, and follow my dreams. I am seventeen years old I just graduated, this year 2004.

Wow that is awesome everyone was enthused by her dreams and aspirations, never forgetting she was only seventeen years old.

After the orientation she was blissful she came home and she told Flaw about the outstanding meeting and felt she had made the right decision.

One day flaw came to Sapphire to ask her if she would mind babysitting while she goes to school. Sapphire did not mind and from that point on she became a babysitter for Flaw. Never knowing she will regret it.

Sapphire had a boyfriend name Peter she loved him so dear, she always came when he needed her no matter what time of day or night.

Baby look I want you to go to college, and farther your education. Look sweet heart you are going to need it. Time is changing it is best while things are still fresh in your mind Said Peter.

Yeah but Baby I going to take a break.

Walking over to Peter massaging his shoulders

Look Honey I know what I am doing.

What is that?

I decided to help Flaw with her two kids. So we planned that I stay out of school for one year, until she can get on her feet, than I will go to school.

Peter jumped up.

No! Heck No! Your taking off from school for her! I bet if it was you she would say forget you, Baby can't you see. She is using you.

Peter walks to the refrigerator to get a cup of orange juice.

Can't you see? You're not fatuitous? I believe you need to go to college now! Look I will pay your way through school, please a couple of thousands aint nothing.

Sapphire starts crying.

Well I really plan on going to school. I just want to help Flaw because I figure. Like, why not.

Look she is going to be done with school and you're going to be just getting started and you're going to looking stupid. That chick is going to have a house and a car and you are going to have nothing. Look. Stop letting her use you. I love you. I will not lie to you, I don't want a woman that don't have nothing, I need someone that can help me when I need it. What if I need help with paying something my girl should be able to help me right?

Peter points to his head.

It's like you being established and having a man that has nothing going for himself, he always is depending on you. And you began to say to yourself. Dag-on man can you do something can you bring something to the table? Look Sapphire I'm not asking you for much I just want you to go to school or get a job, a real job. Watch one day you gone ask that chick for something and she is going to laugh right in your face. Girl this is serious, I hope you listen to what I'm saying to you.

Peter picks up the cup and drinks, with watery eyes.

∧∧∧∧∧∧∧∧∧∧∧∧∧∧∧∧∧∧∧∧∧∧∧∧∧∧

Neosha friend name Summer whom she always call. "the sister I never had" meaning someone that she would confide in as she would do one of her sisters, because the bond she had with her, she knew she could not ever get with one of her older sisters, she was like Sapphire's best friend, Sapphire did not get to close to, too many people. She helped Sapphire with her first job at a theme park.

After getting the job Sapphire called up her boyfriend Peter to tell him the good news.

Hey Honey I have a job. Where? he said.

At a theme park.

Really? Said Peter.

Over the phone she could hear the crackling in his voice.

Baby I knew you could do it.

I knew it.

I love you so much.

Thank you Honey Bun. I love you to.

Sapphire worked on her job for two weeks and was ready to quit. Sapphire barges into Peter's house.

Honey.

Greeting him face to face.

What. Wait a minute; did you just walk in my house? You did not knock; you did not call or say you were coming. And you are just going to barge in my house?

Well, later for what you are saying. I just started my job and I am ready to retire.

Peter laughs so hard bending over holding his stomach.

You just got started.

There is this guy I use to know when I was in junior high school and she had this chick that box, come approach me.

Yeah because he still likes you. He really wants to be with you.

Man he better leave me alone. I not going to have that, I don't even want to fight anymore. I'm finished with High School and I getting ready to start my life and I don't need them in it.

Sapphire begins to cry, in frustration.

Peter walks up to Sapphire and holds her face.

Look at me.

Sapphire looks up.

Yes.

You're pretty and they are all jealous of you. They are so annoying.

I'm starting to hate myself. I don't get it what do they want?

I don't know but I see that you're trying but what are you going to do when you get a real job and you have people hating on you. Are you going to give up? Maybe you're just being tested.

Sapphire stayed on the job as long as she could then she gave up work and went back to babysitting for Flaw. The job was a seasonal position.

∧∧∧∧∧∧∧∧∧∧∧∧∧∧∧∧∧∧

Summer asked Sapphire if she wanted to move down south with her. And Sapphire said no because she did not want to leave Peter alone. All along she could have been chasing opportunities and the agreement was for everyone to pay a certain amount of money for rent and Sapphire was supposed to attend a Performing Arts College a few blocks from the house. But Flaw said she really needed Sapphires help.

Summer told Sapphire.

"Look those are her kids, why are you putting your life on hold for somebody else?"

"I bet she would not do it for you, come on start your new life while you don't have a family. I can help you."

"You will find your husband down south."

"And by the way how old is this guy, your after."

Sapphire never told because she knew Summer would not have agreed with her because of the age gap between the two of them.

In latent dysfunction she told Summer to give her a year. The thing about it Summer wanted Sapphire to leave when she left because she had just graduated College in two-thousand four as well, and was going to start law school. Sapphire stayed behind.

∧∧∧∧∧∧∧∧∧∧∧∧∧∧

Reflections

Sapphire use to come home from work with swollen feet and ankles from standing in the water for so many hours. She use to come to Peter's house crying and he would pick her up when she got to the stairs and carry her the rest of the way into the house.

He would sit her down at the table and massage her feet while she was in great agony. Sapphire would scream as loud as she could that the pain was going up her legs, Peter at times did not know what to do. So he would cry with her as he massaged her feet, wishing he never told her to get a job.

The bone in Sapphires feet would not bend, so he had forced it to bend and the bone had popped. Sapphire gave up fighting with all she had and surrender to the pain and cried. He kept bending it until the joints in both feet became flexible. She cried herself to sleep that night in the chair.

The next morning he picked her up around five o'clock and put her in the bed. Fixed her breakfast, and brought the food over to her singing her name.

Sapphire...

Sapphire...

Sapphire...

Sapphire was too feeble to feed herself so he fed her for three days straight breakfast, lunch and dinner. When he would come home from work he would bring her something while he was out.

In her recovery Peter enjoyed listening to Sapphire tells of make believe stories. At times while they were getting ready for bed he would ask her to tell him a story. While he sit at the edge of the bed massaging her feet, laughing and crying.

No I cannot take from the man that he is but when I learned my worth is when things changed.

Moving on...
This was one of the saddest days of my life him and I was so close;

Prayers do change things! I have a testimony; I am witness of what Jesus brought me out of, that made me more dedicated to him. I want people to see that Jesus is real,

And then... there was a rude awaken!

It was the weekend of Mothers' day it was about sixty-seven degrees. Quin and I was on the phone, she wanted me to go to her University College to visit her. I was also pondering if I should go there or not. I figured it wouldn't interfere with anything, so, I got dressed, and I put on Flaw brown Eco red jacket with blue jeans and put on my brown and black snack skin shoes. I did my hair, I put my hair in flat twist and put the rest into a pony tail with my burgundy and black weave, I put on my butterfly ear rings, glossed my lips, put on my purse and was ready to go. I'm five seven hash brown complexion with dreadlocks, down to my shoulders, and have a demanding look.

Flaw friend Ruth was over and she needed a ride to the train station. My train was at one-thirty p.m. I arrived there at one o'clock. First I went to the ticket booth to purchase my tickets, than I went out to the deck it was crowded I paste back and forth on the deck I had a little time left before my train came. So I ran down stairs and purchased a toasted bagel with cream cheese and a fruit Toppa strawberry kiwi drank, it came up to three dollars and twenty-five cents.

I ran upstairs, my leg was so tired. I slowed down a little walked up the three steps to the deck, there was this man that kept on gazing at me, as I paste back n' forth. I began to ponder to myself why is the man gazing at me, he wasn't the only one. So I proceeded to ponder what I was going to do when I get to my destination.

My legs started to get tired from standing so I found a seat on the bench, I sat there knowing I was looking good, I healed my head up with confidence, I crossed my legs holding my purse with a firm grip on my lap.

The man that was gazing at me began to walk closer; I looked over at him he came closer, so I was thinking to myself please don't talk to me! Please don't ask me any questions, and don't come by me!

He walked over and stood next to the bench I was sitting on and he was talking on the phone. He was about six feet tall, brown skin with glasses he really looked like a nerd blue Jeans that was faded with a white T-shirt, navy blue dirty timberland boots looked like he was doing construction and wore a fitted.

His game was corny I peeped it from the start he stood in front of me and talked loud so he could have all of my attention on him. So I looked around trying not to give him what he desired.

Then he said. Dang who is this fine young lady, come sit next to me?

I thought to myself that was lame, that was the lowest approach I ever had. But I went with the flow to see where his head was at.

I smiled, and said Hi.

With your sexy self dang! He said.

So what is your name? He said.

Sapphire. I said.

He said. Sapphire. Dang girl I know you're not single."

He said to his friend. Dang yo this gal looks fine I'm going to call you back.

He handed me his cell phone. I said. What who is it?

My friend wants to talk to you." He said.

I'm guessing he wanted to hear my voice, so I took the phone.

Hi, how are you doing? His friend said.

I'm all right and yourself." I said.

"I'm good." I said.

I gave him back the phone. I gazed at him checking his profile, for a while I gazed into his face. He was looking like he was getting hypnotize while gazing into my brown eyes. The more he gazed into my face it seemed like he was reading my mind.

Alright I'll call you when I get there, because this girl looks so dang good.

As he stood in front of me he began to ask me.

Where are you going? He said.

How about you? I asked.

He then stated that his cousin was having a birthday party, at a bar asking if I could bring my girls.

I agreed to do so.

Then we exchanged numbers.

Okay this is my final time asking you Do you or do you not want to stay? Asked shabby.

I don't want to stay. Neosha replied.

Okay. Then Shabby went back to his friends and told Neosha's reply.

DS, Covet, and Shabby got in the car. Neosha stayed seated in the back of the vehicle on the right side, Shabby sat on the other side, Covet sat in the front on the passenger's side and DS got behind the wheel.

DS said "I don't want to drive. Who ever want to drive can drive."

DS said Neosha why don't you drive.

No. Declared she, the first thing that come to her mind was getting pulled over for some reason and losing her license before she could get them. Also she felt frighten.

Each insisted that she do so, so she voiced how she was feeling.

No I'm not driving!

Why? They asked.

Because I'm scared.

All man, I don't feel like driving. D.S said and he took the wheel.

Neosha prayed an inner prayer for the Lord to bless that they would have a safe ride on their journey.

DS made a right turn out of the complex. As soon as he began to make a right on the main road, there was a police car in the middle of the street, construction work was on, and so he had to make a detour. They had to take another route. DS sped a little, but everything was okay. He turned on to the bridge. The whole time Neosha was praying and thanking Jesus for blessing they made it this far.

He made a right on to the main street, everything was okay, and they were getting closer to their destination. As they were getting close to the jug handle, DS decides he wants to speed up.

Shabby can you please tell him to slow down? Neosha demanded.

Nah it's alright I got you.

We do this all the time relax. Shabby insisted.

DS suddenly began to speed going fifty to sixty miles per hour. Neosha yelled slow down!

I'm getting scared.

Shabby calmly said "it's okay ain't nothing going to happen to you."

DS loses control of the car.

BAM! He rides on the curb.

Neosha was yelling at him and saying.

"Oh My God!"

"Oh MY God!"

Forget this I'll walk tell him to stop the car opening the door to get out. While DS was trying to grip control of the stirring wheel, all of a sudden the back end of the car goes backwards into a ditch.

The car flipped. Neosha yelled to the top of her lungs.

"OH MY GOD!"

"OH MY GOD!"

The back window had shattered. The first thing the crossed her mind is that I'm going to die.

Oh God I don't know what to do!

Lord help me please! Just when she thought it was over and everybody was safe the car flipped again. Everything seemed as if it was slow motion, she couldn't believe it.

She yelled. MOM! DADDY! SOMEBODY HELP!

OH MY GOD I'M SCARED!

SOMEBODY HELP! HELP!

Fear she began to feel all over. She hit her head on the ceiling; she began to call on Jesus.

Covet said. Oh my God this girl is loud.

Shut up, you are hurting my ears!

WHAT! WHAT! WHERE GOING TO DIE!

DS and Covet kept telling her to shut up.

Neosha closed her eyes; she got humble for a minute and prayed to the Lord.

Lord if this is my time to go I will I want to have kids and get married. Hell crossed her mind. She knew her soul was not right with God, her heart was racing it felt like she was having a heart attack, and her mind wasn't at ease.

She asked Jesus to "forgive her for all of her sins." As tears rolled down her face promising Jesus that she'll make peace with those who trespassed against her. She pled in agony

Lord I'll do your will.

Please do not call me home I don't want to burn.

The car flipped again.

This time she hit her head so hard her skull had cracked everything rattled, dizziness appeared.

Not knowing what to do the yelling immediately ceased her body was now feeble, for moments there was strength it had all fled.

Pondering in mind that Jesus had giving up on her.

She replied again. Jesus forgive me I want to make a change my life. I want to live for you.

As the vehicle flipped shabby fell on Neosha's hip. Feeble in all nothing could be done.

Suddenly again hitting her head almost knocking her out; she had opened the car before it began to flip it was the same door she was thrown out of. Hallucinating the car will blow up. "Jesus was the burning bush." she was thrown on to big rocks; it was more than a fall or a throw it was a dive on to the rocks head first.

Her head was inside her shoulders, num and intoxicated, discombobulated, her thinking was slow she was broken, Impaired, movement and stiff.

In her feeble dedicated communication to Jesus she pondered, I rather die than suffer in hollow vast state of thinking she heard sounds from covet and DS they was saying to shabby in a sore voice. Shabby are you alright?

A yo Shabby are you alright?

In an afflicted voice Shabby replied yeah Mon I'm alright check on Neosha.......

Yo man I don't know Covet responded she look bad. She looks dead.

Shabby began to call out Noesha… Noesha….

His voice was remote. Are you alright?

Talk to me.

It sound as if he was crying, she couldn't answer.

Noesha could barely move or breathe, internally her head was aching. Ribs was hurting, pelvis was hurting everything in her was at a miserable state.

Her heart felt like it was beating out side of her body, all that she could ponder on was perishing, pain never felt this way before. Tears rolled down her cheeks, trying to repress her cry. Tears were a burden, not really wanting to breathe, feeling the plus behind the ribs the beating muscle. The flow of oxygen was not normal. Every breath felt like her last.

Before her mind went she again asked Jesus to forgive her, and tell my family and friends not to cry."

Be strong tell everybody I love them bless everyone. Than her eyes shut."

The fellows she was with took her arms and legs. With the miniature strength she had she uttered in affliction.

"No Please, Leave me.

"It hurt."

They tried to comfort her with words like.

Noesha you're going to be alright.

Then she lost consciousness. When she opened her eyes again the miniature vision she had was hazy.

They had put her in a white car that belong to Deuces and lent they are husband and wife they are best friends to DS, Covet, Shabby and Buch. Their house is where the driver of the car was headed the destination was less than a mile away. The guys had driven her to the hospital.

* * * * * * * * *

Neosha was given reappearance; it was her mother who had passed away when she was ten years old. She was in white garment, her mother was saying in a loud voice.

"Neosha!"

Come on Neosha!'

You can make it!

Neosha was able to give heed to her mother's voice, while she was in the state of code blue.

No. No. Mommy no.

I miss you. Daddy need you, Mommy everybody miss you.

Why did you have to go?

She said baby it was my time to go, I live through ya'll, you, all my kids I never left I'm still here!

Every time Neosha took her last breath her mother would call her name.

Neosha wake up! Neosha wake up!

Neosha then came back to life, and she stood talking to her mother she began to cry;

Neosha don't weep I'm alright, just get saved!

Get the Holy Ghost!

God is coming back, when he comes I want to be with all my kids and Frank, tell everybody I love them.

I'm doing fine, I'm not suffering anymore.

Neosha proceeded to weep; suffering while tears streamed down her face, each tear gave trail memories of mourning.

Neosha could barely embrace how much she was blissful to see her mother's face.

People are so cruel, Mommy please.

When Neosha was driven back to reality her body was in so much agony. The little vision she had was so hazy, the lights were bright people was moving close to her face, doctors was putting up fingers, no matter what she couldn't speak only thing she was able to do was gaze.

What's your name?

How old are you?

What happened?

Suddenly Neosha went back into code blue.

This time was her mother and a angle. Neosha embraced to her mother that she missed her.

Neosha it's going to be alright you are here for a reason.

What is it?

In what ways show me, tell me how.

Help the people they need your guidance, you're a leader, they need you.

Guide your sisters and brothers.

Then reality came, they was shocking her body.

The fourth time she felt like she was going to be with her mother, internally she found joy. Her mother than appeared in the clouds and they were reaching for one another. Neosha tried her best to grab her hand but every time she thought she had it she didn't.

Neosha get up!

Neosha get up!

Wake up! Wake Up!

You got to push on through life it's not ease I know.

You have to set roles for people; God blessed you with many talents.

She began to call them out as if they were toffees.

You even have talents the have not been revealed to you yet. God is going to bless you he'll never go astray, just remain in church. Learn

Learn to forgive I know it can be a little complicated sometimes but do it.

You know church is where I would be, keep on praying, keep on striving.

Okay. Okay.

Neosha proceeded to reach for her hand but never touched it.

Her mother looked so beautiful and pure. She began to fade.

Neosha kept calling her name, she just kept going.

Yelling No! No! Mommy you said you'll never leave me.

Her final words were help Shane (he is Neosha's little brother) show him the way.

Then she vanished.

* * * * * * * * *

When they got to the hospital they said the car was high jacked and she was fighting some girls and they beat her with a bat. They did not know their names. (But they switched Neosha's by calling her something else). She was unconscious bleeding from the head and covered in blood her skull was fractured in six places with major head trauma, in latent dysfunction she lost her memory in time it was gradually regained.

* * * * * * * * *

The next day Neosha was not allowed to eat nor drink, doctors and specialists were running dynastic test on her, she was bleeding internally. Days later Family and friends came to visit, they were ready for war. Veronicas, Victoria, Dina, Flaw and Summer.

Veronicas asked. Neosha you'll got jumped?

Neosha frailly said no. Was car accident.

If it was a car accident, then why did they say you'll got robbed, beat up and they took the car?

I'm telling the truth alright.

I really don't believe you.

Overtly she cried. Victoria was dressed in blue sweat pants with a loose t-shirt prepared for battle. After they had left Neosha sister Zola came.

What happened?

Accident.

Whatchu mean it was a accident.

Car accident.

I thought you was jumped, I was prepared to fight.

Shabby walked in the room with his head tilled to the right side.

Mon ya okay Mon?

Don't know hurt.

So who are you? Asked Zola.

I'm her friend we helped her, Mon she almost died.

Story I Never Want To Forget

Last year two thousand six my pastor her mother and I went to the south to visit their kin. While I was down there Summer had came to the hotel we were staying at that night, and she picked me up.

We had gone to a Reggae concert in the south. It was nice outside the concert started at one o'clock. He sang four songs, I danced to the rhythm, all eyes was on me, I was feeling really good. At three o'clock the party ended.

I asked for his autograph and his brother for the same. (They are both reggae artist.)

Two days later my friend and I went to see them again. This time and I got up close and personal. I sat on his coach in the hotel room and asked him questions.

I said Five months ago I was in a real bad car accident. The car flipped four times and I was thrown from the car.

My neck was almost broken, my ribs were fracture in two places, my pelvis was fracture and I had head trauma. Both of my lungs collapsed and I was resuscitated seven times.

And he said you look good for that to happen to you.

I said with my head down reminded of the tragedy in my head. Yeah but I don't understand it.

What. What do you mean. He asked

You know how God moves, and how he allows us to go through so much.

Yeah I understand.

Jesus! He said.

He said it with so much might, I felt like I had to turn back and get something right with him. But this time I couldn't let go of God.

just listened as if he had all day.

I began to cry, all the things I repressed from what occurred the verbal abuse had gotten to my heart where I even questioned my begin of who I am and where would I go from here.

So I turned my head.

Why are you crying, it seems like something is bothering you, be free with me, look I have all day. Let it out. What happened to you was good because you got out.

I put my head down; I was taken by the moment and flash backs flashed.

You know no matter what people say to you if something happened to you, it happened don't let nobody take that from you. Those things you cherish are your jewels. Don't give it to swine, selfish greedy people, because they will leave you with nothing. They will make you cry and not wipe one tear, they will set you back and they would go forward. These people stay away from leave them alone.

Yeah I have seen a lot of them. But it is something you're not telling me. He said.

Life is too hard.

I can't take it, it stings.

What he said.

Everything, my bones have been broken for five months. I can't wait until it is all over.

Look let it all out if you don't it will make you sick, you may not have somebody that will listen to you but I will.

Okay. Because of the car accident I was in, with these guys it wasn't my car or anything but these guys made believe to me that we were friends but they're intent was to kill me.

My families talk s about me like a dog. At one point everything was all good now they turned against me.

How do you feel now, because I feel you are relieved?

I feel a little better. But do you think things will change?

He began to cry and hugged me, saying everything is going to be alright. Come back home to Jesus he wants to use you. It's your turn to let go."

We both cry together.

I have never gotten that from no one, with everyone else it was like get over it! Whatever you went through, whatever happen to you o 'well. But here I had this famous person, someone who is popular to show me some empathy. I appreciated every moment of it. Some body was willing to come to my level.

Jesus loves you. He said. When He spoke it he meant it.

I said Jesus what, I can't believe it he is so mad at me, that's why I am going through this.

He said maybe you shouldn't feel that way, just say thank you Jesus. You look fine you look good.

He said I heard of you, you have taught a lot of people.

Some people from his entourage knew me.

Jesus is going to use you. He said.

The questions I asked him were so well thought because I did not want him to know about my speech impairment as being so bad.

But every now and then he would hear something in my speech, it was uncontrollable.

I had to let it go I said.

I have something to confess.

He looked over at me.

Your music is amazing it really touched me. I was swaying at first, but then I started to praise God and I couldn't stop the spirit it was moving.

The main part about your song is when you said the hook.

"Life goes on. Life goes on; on… life goes on everyday another babies born can't see the sunlight in the dark."

That made me cry harder because I know I am living in darkness without Jesus being inside me. I'm Christian we call it the walking dead when one don't have the Holy Ghost t on the inside, because the Spirit of Jesus is light.

Hi brother came into the room.

When are you going to write your book?

I don't know. I said.

I want you to write a book, 'cause if anything happen you got your own proof.

I believe what you say, you are very funny.

We both chuckled.

Ya'll make me feel so good.

I was in a tragedy and being around ya'll make me feel much better.

"Can I do a video to your song children crying out for love?"

What chu gonna do?

I can picture little children sitting around you, while you are sitting on a rock saying children are crying out for love.

But I have to get back with you with the vision.

That particular song made me think of my problems as being nothing. My heart is heavy right now and this song made me think.

When I seen you it touched me to I have never been able to turn my head, see look I can turn it.

I could never jump up and down but I did.

Who do you think did it? Jesus.

God, I believe it was Jesus. It was his power.

Do you know you are a good story teller?

What everybody say that.

It's a gift from God, and I want you to be my ghost writer. He said.

I understand, but I'm on my way out. I'm about to die, I am sick unto death I can't even stand that long my knees began to buckle. I am still weak.

There manager came in bringing food.

Fish, rice and beans he offered me some and I said no I don't eat.

He said that's why you're so feeble, when was the last time you ate?

I couldn't say, I did not know.

So he offered again, and I said alright.

I said put some on my hand.

He did and I felt like I could think for a change.

It tasted so good.

He recommended that I eat with him. I said I did not want to eat all of his food. He said no please eat.

I could not recall the last time I ate he offered me the fork, but I did not know how to hold it. His last unremarkable word that night was your amazing.

The things that I carried out in mind that I will not forget is when They "said go to College and God will help you, no matter what don't give up. You are very strong minded. Don't give up, Jesus loves you."

Also

I would like to see you again.

All she could remember saying is, if ever your story is true stick with it. No matter what they say no matter what they do. The truth is they lied and I am here because of Jesus. Those people left me for dead; they did not want me to be here."

* * * * * * * * *

One day Neosha was over a relative house, she had just finished her hair. There was an unusual thought that kept crossing her mind, no way in mind could she grasp the conception, it was revelation time. The vivid and bubbling thoughts of Hell graviton her mind.

Jesus had come back for his saints and Neosha sat right beside a male angle, all things was visual as foretold in the Holy Bible prophesies had come to pass. Planes were falling out of the sky, gnashing of teeth people that didn't have faith started to believe, but it was too late.

He showed her demons that God had in chains unto the Day of Judgment be released, torturing the people, everything was in kazoo. Fornicators, adulators, robbers people trying to kill themselves but they could not die. The earth was raining fire people prayed, prayers that could not help they did all they could.

Neosha called on Jesus in her mind. Instantly she began to repent.

Jesus please forgive me for all of my sins, sorry for everything that was not right in your sight. Neosha had brought new books and the spirit of the angle said write. She had brought new books so she began to write everything that had come to mind, all that was revealed was a bad outcome. Mother against daughters, fathers against sons, Kids having babies that world was so corrupt. Seeing all this she again called on Jesus out of a loud cry.

Jesus declared warn my people! He had sent prophets, preachers, ministers, saints, he called them all and said good work thy good and faithful servants. There was a gulf between Heaven and Hell. When looking down she saw people suffering. That's when she wanted to give up everything and surrender to God. The world was burning forever, she fell to her face. The voice of the angle spoke saying no matter how much you don't like a person, you never turn down the hand that trying to know more about Jesus. You are to love your neighbor as thy self. Trembling came through her body.

Through that vision Jesus was renewing her again, washing away all of the sins she had.

Redemption
Yes you can readme me from my past
Yes I am so happy!
No more will I have to mourn
Yes you emancipated me!
No more will I have to look back and regret!
This Sunday I plan to give myself to you
I want to be a changed person
Yes Jesus you rearranged me!

Tears fall on the earth
To nature the land
For the grass to grow taller
Leaves to change its colors
Tears fall on the earth
Healthy, grateful, and happy
a lot of things happen for a reason,
Confused no more!
Life is given from God.

This poem is talking about how everything has its place.
It tells how nature change and how us people
Change and I predicted redemption.
Life he gives because the guys I was with almost kilt me,
To cover themselves how the rain pours is symbolized the tears.

My Prayer
Jesus a lot of things is hard to explain
And hard to understand
Jesus I know you will guide me
Sometimes I get confused and don't know what to do
I don't want people to dislike me or go astray
Lord please bless me with understanding

Things was crossing my mind that were troubling me
Things said were far fetch
And I didn't want my own people to go astray
So I was asking Jesus to give me understanding
"What's going on?"

Why do we cry?
To clean the frustration from our eyes so we can
See more clearly
And get a break through from the outside in
You can cure me
Why do we cry?
To release the hindering emotions
And gain understanding
And see you are the way out of the desert island
And to see clearly
I was asking Jesus why we cry, every day I would
Cry until I got sick, but I wouldn't allow anyone to see
And I was answering my own self
Saying the things I said
And showing people that Jesus is the truth and the light

Jesus Speak to me
Many see some things wrong with me
Jesus says there is nothing wrong
My child look up to me
I can deliver you from all
I know your strength and weakness
Stand tall
My child believe in me
Life is everlasting
My child
I see you cry, I know your weak, that's okay
You can cry, look up to me

Your faith is strong don't allow anything
to anyone to tell you other
My child look up to me
Keep the faith everything will fall into its proper place!

Destiny
The past I leave behind
Today I must go on
The future is my destiny
I put you first above all
Because I need to make a change
Jesus only you can change me
Yes, I know you said to never give up
And lean on you and trust

Question
When will they understand?
When will I see the light?
When will I learn?
When will this pain surcease?
When will this all go away?

I've been through a struggle
Waiting for justice
I can't wait until it's completely over
So I can be happy all over again?

LET GO LET GOD!

FAITH
Yes, you redeemed me from my past
Yes, I'm so happy
No more will I have to mourn

Yes, you freed me
No more will I have to look back

Jesus took away, all of my pain,
And I received happiness
I'm graceful I see the light
Now all I give is love and
Encouraging words,
I'm cured from my sickness,
It was Jesus that carried me!

* * * * * * * * *

Neosha began to reminisce on her past afflictions and said too many.

I'm going to someday put it all in a book to help others get through their infirmities. The book was to be candid and just.

This chapter is called redemption, after all those years Jesus the genesis came and she knew there was nothing to continually be repressed, the hurdles are now be coming track fields, now she's able to run, walk and take things for what it is.

The nurses took good care of me. The guys never brought to suffer face what really occurred. Family and friends would come to visit me at the hospital and ask me what happened. And all I could say was it was an accident. But every time I said accident it meant car accident.

People started to feel like I was covering things up but were really out of mind. All along there was a snare and had no inkling they were setting me up for failure.

I suffered long from silence. I say now to myself speak or forever hold my piece.

At times I was in the state of solitary recalling the incident. Dr. Stephen had come into the room and asked.

There was no longer an expression for me as I wept coldly sore. Everyone has gone away from me all I had been through nobody, seemed as if anyone really wanted to be bothered there was a great misconception to the rule of expressions.

The doctor hesitantly told me you're gonna have problems like retardation, your bones will heal, that will take time. You have a lot of head trauma things are not going to be the same, you was hit hard. Both lungs had clasped there going to be okay. Your heart was torn ten layers of tissues you lost a lot of your heart, you almost died, you will have to drink a lot of water to flush out the damaged tissues. There is a strong possibility you can't have kids. If so you'll have complications, you might have a high risk pregnancy or possibly bleed to death.

But the most vial thing is that you.

You're here for a reason again he asked what happened.

A crime has been committed don't let these guys get away with it. Then he left.

I recalled how frozen I was, I was so hurt, all I could do was cry. Why me?

Gaining foreknowledge on the issues that was to come.

Therapy

The therapist came in to do physical therapy. The therapist had come in with her an intern.

Kylee was the rapist name the intern was name was Amber.

Kylee had brought in a walker, than she called for a wheelchair. Neosha begged her if she could have another opportunity to walk. She tried bending one of her knees but they were too stiff, they could not bend.

She said I will have to break your knees or they might have to amputate them because you might have to be in a wheelchair for the rest of your life.

Neosha cried sorely because it had seemed to her that the nurse refused to give her a chance. Inwardly Neosha started crying and praying. She herself could not move her legs.

Kylee put her leg in the air and the right knee didn't bend, she told her that there was a problem, she than did the same to the other one but it bent.

Neosha wept historically it felt like she did not have any consideration for her fractured pelvis, but prayer do chance things.

Kylee pushed her began to push her right leg back and it took a while but it bent.

Neosha yelled to the top of her lungs!

She bent it back three than four times. Enduring a large amount of pain the nurse had left her for that day, than came back two days later. She bent the leg back and forth until it bent without a problem.

Than it came time to walk Neosha had to sit up and move to the edge of the bed. She tried placing her feet to the floor, just when she thought she had it she fell to the floor. There was a loud crack she was so frail, they helped her into the bed, putting her back into the proper position. Neosha prayed inwardly, Kylee she to have given up on her and said.

You won't be able to walk again; you will have to be in the wheelchair for the rest of your life." Then she walked out.

Neosha cried to the Jesus and begged him to deliver her, and bless that she will be able to walk again, vowing that she will never sin any more, I will do your will, and forever abide in your word.(The bible) and do your will the mite of faith she had in her prayer Jesus blessed.

The next time the therapist came in the room. Neosha prayed to Jesus the whole time, this time with more confidence with no doubt in herself. Feebly she stood and fell the lady fret; she refused to chance it again.

Kylee told her to sit back on the bed, Neosha did not even know at the time her hip was out of place, she tried but the ambition she had she knew she could not give up. Kylee moved the walker closer to her Kylee and said.

If you don't get it this time, then were not going to try again.

This time Neosha went to the power house outwardly saying the name of Jesus. Every step of the way she said "Jesus," "Jesus" she gradually stood up more. Every time she did something she said thank you Jesus. Boldly feeling mildly better for that moment the mind she was emancipated from the afflictions she had, and thank God she stepped, wiggling and focused, proceeding saying Jesus. She had it, every day after that she took step by step. The lady was startled she said it was a miracle. Neosha did physical therapy until it was time to go home. (As she breathes she was hooked on to an oxygen machine but faith carried her.)

* * * * * * * * *

Life Goes On....

Neosha pondering to within how she was blessed when she endured hardship no one truly to share it with, because backs were now turned, constantly battling the odds of unfixed ends All solitude saying "can I get a witness" and all she had was torn, she finally reached the point to state "LIFE GOES ON....."

Neosha which is me ShTruth Poetry is with a new mindset, that people know, but don't know.

DIARY

The truth will reveal itself, but everything was kept secret. Almost lost my life over their foolishness.
I learned my lesson that took one time

He healed me I got my health back Jesus heard my cry faith is what carried me.

This one was the hardest best Jesus is real

Watch what you pray for and watch what you say.

Every day is a risk, mind what you say don't rush your life.

I count my steps things could have been worst but Jesus delivered me.

I'm following my heart and living out my dreams!

I believe in myself

Jesus revealed what he has revealed and brought this faded picture to color.

I gradually shrug my shoulders not saying forget about it but to God be the glory.

Everything has it purpose, everything has its place.
Car accidents occur every day some people are blessed and can walk away. And some seem to be less fortunate and become traumatized from the event of a breath taking situation.

Go to church and ask Jesus to bless and he will.

Pray without ceasing

Know who is who there are sheep in wolves clothes

Always keep a smile on your face no matter how things get

Life is too short to hold grudges Forgive

Trust me you will feel better

I almost died because of the people I affiliated myself with "be careful."

I hope this book inspired you to live out your dreams
I almost gave up the things I love most
Writing, drawing, and doing hair

Just stay positive don't listen to everything people say.
(Kind of know what to listen to and kind of know what to ignore)

Live out your dreams!

Bring them to reality!

Wake up and live!

Peace!

To everything there is a season, and a time
a purpose under the heaven:
A time to heal; a time to break down, and a time to build up;
A time to weep, and a time to laugh; a time
to mourn, a time to cast away stones,
A time to get, and a time to lose;
Ecclesiastes chapter 3
I know that, whatsoever God doeth, it shall be forever
Ecclesiastes chapter 3:14

* * * * * * * * *

Favor is deceitful and beauty is vain knowing wisdom is better than rubies. And content with a virtuous friend.

After months of afflictions and infirmities that are incomparably complicated to diminish the extreme pressures of life. After the horrifying moment of the undeniable tragedy Neosha is now faint. Everything she once had is now vanished her health, independent thinking, disorderly movement of her body, no longer stable with a sound mind. To think precisely, everything's changing after having so many people she could rely on she now has no one. Stiff hands no one seems to give, many seem disappointed that she still lives after expecting the worst. As she gradually try's to speak not too many endure patience but those who come around privately to lay snares to contradict everything she once believed in.

Neosha ponder in solitude

Who do I have?

Who can I now turn to?

Neosha began to attend church more often as she sit in the pews, every-time she hears the name Jesus it's like a new trumpet that sounds in the life of darkness, that bring-est forth eternal light and unconditional love in life.

"Repent! You must get the Holy Ghost if you plan to live eternally with Jesus! Come on church you have got to make it. These are the last of the last days without his spirit you are none of his. This thing is serious it's time to get on board Jesus is coming back sooner than you think, time is winding up. Jesus loves you without love you cannot please God."

Every Sunday she attends a Pentecostal Apostolic church where they do not sugar code the truth. As the unadulterated word of God was preached Neosha began to grow a connection with Jesus, faith cometh by hearing and by hearing the word of God. It is also written how you can hear without a preacher. Church became first hand Neosha could barely read let alone she could hardly pronounce words with proper speech.

Jesus began to open her mind manifesting his self to her; inquisitive questions arose in her mind.

Jesus where are my friends the people I have fought for and ran with for all these years?

I have nothing people are so fake they only want to be around when I was like them, and when I had more going for myself. Jesus I see now that you are all that I have please increase my faith I recall my experience in my last day, please Jesus I don't want to go back help me please. I will forsake everyone just to have a closer walk with you.

As Neosha poured out her heart and mind to Jesus she began to open up, there was a voice crying out in the wilderness, she was making a way for Jesus to pour out his spirit in her, but she was still feeble in her infirmity. Jesus revealed what the end was going to be for those who would perished without the Holy Ghost recognizing that if Jesus speared not the angles that were in Heaven, he was not going to spear any one that was not in him.

Every day she would weep saying to herself.

I know I'm going to die, I know when I die I'm going to Hell. Jesus I need the Holy Ghost I don't want to die in my sins, only you can save me, help me Jesus please whatever it takes I don't want to burn for eternity, I believe there is a Heaven and a Hell. Jesus whatever you tell me to say or do as long as you're with me, I will do it I need your help. Without you I'm nothing my life is a as grass. Jesus all the labor I have done was vain because I was not living for you, every-time I went to church I always thought of what I was going to do when it was over, I did not pay my tithes I did not do all of your will. I see it now you speared my life for a reason, what was it for?

Here I am Lord Use me as you see fit. I surrender to you Jesus all of my friends and family have left me I don't care as much anymore if I have to I'll walk alone just fill me with your holy spirit. Neosha began to cling more to the bible and the instructions of her Pastor,

Pastor Ivory. Recommend that she should, read acts 2:38 and read psalms 70 every night also read psalms 91, you need to get in the word get serious with God, it's a reason for you being here I don't know exactly what it is, but I thank God for you. This Holy Ghost is serious, you gonna need it like the bible said. Be real, be for real.

Every day she would try to read, but her only dilemma was that she could not read so every time the church doors were open she would be present, helping... Neosha wasn't much of a cook but she helped, in cleaning she even became responsible enough to become her Pastor's armor bearer. One way she taught herself how to read was when she was in sunday school and bible study and she would read along with the instructor and ask questions even though she had a hard time speaking with a speech impairment, as she spoke everyone in the class word try to map out what she was trying to say. Gradually they began to make a game out of it.

It was a Sunday morning at Church, the children were in their class and the adults were in their class. Each class had a breaking down of the bible for each level to comprehend the bible better, in the adult class there was ten people attending,

(These things that Neosha was going through went on for a month then finally she gave up Sunday school and only attended regular church service. Pastor Ivory gave her a bible with words in giant print, she cherished it and always brought it to church and everywhere she went. When the Preacher of that hour brought forth the word she followed along. The Pastor always had someone to find which part of the bible she was reading from. Neosha did not give up hope at times when she was home she would open her bible find which part the Preacher read from trying to recite what she heard every day she would do that. Her greatest dilemma was that no one wanted to teach her at home to read, folks would say she is too old not to know how to read, she is just faking and would persist that no one was to help and that she could figure it out herself. So she learned not to lean on people for guidance or for help when she needed it, tremendous amount of her focus was on Jesus, there was something about that name that gave her hope for what she had to face.)

∧∧∧

Zina "the worrier"

For months on in, it was going on two years Neosha was attentive to herself, she'd learned her distance. Pastor Ivory had planned a trip to Detroit Michigan to visit her family her mother Shena persist that this would be a great trip also declaring that she needed to get away from family and friends. They were too judgmental and it would and eventually tarnish her mind paralyzing her individual thinking. Zina that resided in another state known as a childhood friend gives Neosha a call.

Ring! Ring! Ring!

Pastor Ivory picks up the telephone.

Hello!

Hi this is Zina can I please speak to Neosha.

One second, Neosha the phone!

Neosha comes out of the bathroom after taking a shower, placing her belongings on the bed.

Here the phone, reaching her hand out for her to get it.

WHAT! WHO IS THAT!

Hello who's calling?

Zina.

WHAT ARE YOU SERIOUS?

NOBODY CALLS ME, I'M SHOCKED.

Neosha walks over to the phone with a startled face.

YES.

Yes? Girl stop playing how are you doing? I haven't spoken to you in a long time.

YES I KNOW SO, YOU HOW ARE YOU?

Girl I'm in school, I'm just beginning my first semester.

MY GOODNESS SO WHAT MAKES YOU WANT TO CALL ME NOBODY CALLS ME WHEN I'M HOME HARDLY ANYONE TALKS TO ME. I'M JUST THERE FLAW JUST GO AROUND CALLING ME BAZZAR. BUT I JUST LOOK AT HER LIKE SHE IS FATUIOUS.

Look calm down it's me I can tell you are shocked relax I'm not going to hurt you, I don't bite.

Zina chuckles, than Neosha in latent dysfunction she laughs. Neosha begins to cry.

I CAN'T BELIEVE I'M GETTING A PHONE CALL everybody left my side. When I say I have nobody. I mean I have no one, people just judge me the children are the main ones that talk to me. I felt like I was about to go back in the rehabilitation center

What! Noesha what do you mean the rehabilitation center.

I WAS PUT IN THE REHAB because I could take the pressures of life; I began to feel like what they were calling me was true. FLAW WAS THE MAIN ONE she was always putting ideals 'bout me in my family minds now they are turned against me. Man all I feel is torment I am in an opposition of things that has nothing to do with me, now I am being punished I can't understand why?

I know man that car accident a yo man it was that car accident. That's why everyone changed on you, I even hate it myself. Said Zina.

MAN I FEEL PEOPLE WOULD HAVE BEEN MORE CONTENT IF I HAD PARISHED. I DON'T CARE WHAT NO ONE HAS TO SAY! Said Neosha.

A yo man I care I've been always getting up crying late at night praying that you would be alright a yo you was sick. I hated the way you looked some people had jokes until they saw you, all I could do was cry, I was frightened. A yo I hate those guys, why did they have to do that? Said Zina.

A YO YOUR ENEMIES PLAY YOUR FRIENDS TO they got away big time, I can't even believe it happened to me, I suffered long I would wake up every day hoping that God would call me home. I was always in agony no matter what I said people would not listen to me. They would ask me now do you remember what happened and I would not respond, because they were being sarcastic like I literally planed not to say anything, I now feel like a person who have been shot five times than being asked what happened? Who are the guys what was the argument about? And the body is dead. Said Neosha.

Zina laughs.

There is no response.

I'm telling you be cautious who you make your friends people will turn on you, why because they have a change of heart. I would have never thought that would have happened to me. I truly hated myself every day I would wonder what was that for.

Yeah but if things happened the other way would you still have kept them your friend? Said Zina.

Yeah maybe but they would not like how I would have sued them, look at me now there is no telling how the future is going to be for me. I probably can't have children because of their foolishness.

Neosha breaks down crying, than Zina cries.

A yo man I should have never left you; I feel I should have been there. I should have held back that car. I should have been there; they should have never gotten to you.

MAN PEOPLE CAN FEEL HOW THEY WANT NOW WHEN I LOOK BACK THERE INTENTION WAS FOR ME TO DIE, THEY WERE TRYING TO KILL ME!

THEY TOOK ME TO THE HOSPITAL AND SAID THAT I WAS BEATEN WITH A BAT WHEN IT WAS A CAR ACCIDENT. CHIEF THEY WOULD DO ANYTHING! I TRUST NONE OF THEM I DON'T CARE IF WE NEVER TALK AGAIN. I TRY MY BEST NOT TO HATE; IN THIS CASE its HARD JESUS WAS THERE! JESUS DELIVERED ME! THEY WERE WORKING FOR THE DEVIL. I feel like David when he asked God to deliver him out of the hands of his enemies.

In psalm seventy he said let them be ashamed and confounded that seek after my soul. The devil was on his job that night. He knew who exactly who to use, I'm not having it I don't care what no one has to say. Anybody that takes their side is against me!

Yo this aint my battle it's the Lords Jesus is gonna have to finish this battle for me, I can't do this all by myself if self is in the way than Jesus can't do what he said he would do. I pray someday I get a case if it be God's will. Truly he has blessed me in my health and I won't take it back, I just could not do it myself. Sorry I know I keep repeating myself but God Jesus Christ is mighty and God over everything. Before I went in the bathroom I was reading the holy bible the King James Version in the book of ecclesiastics it says "there is no new thing under the sun that which is done is that which shall be." What has happened has been here before, all man's labor under the sun is vain so there will come a time when everything shall melt away." I take Jesus at his word he is coming back, sooner than we think whether we are ready or not he is coming back for his people.

So you believe everything that happened, happened for a reason? Said Zina.

Yes!

So like what are you doing for yourself now, are you just going to keep on reading the bible?

Zina girl I don't just read the bible. I also attend church I am my Pastors armor bearer.

What is that? I have never heard of that before.

A armor bearer is someone who attend to the needs of the Pastor, the person may brings him or her a cup of water or just something to drink, the person may carry their Pastor armor which is the robe, coat, or bible, have you heard of the saying you have to put on the whole armor of God?

I don't know. I go to church sometimes but I've never gotten much into it. Tell me what it is. Said Zina.

I'm referring to the natural which is the breast plate, helmet, shield, with the whole armor of God. And there also is a spiritual side to it which is to keep us protected from the enemy. I surrender all to Jesus without him I would be nothing. And I stress the fact. I'm very active in the church I just, just learned how to read I literally taught myself, nobody helped me all they did was make fun of me. I remember when I was over your Grandparents house and I asked you if you could teach me how to read and teach me my math and you said you aint teaching no grown women nothing. That junk hurt me I felt like I had no one. ALL THAT MY FAMILY DO IS JUDGE ME. FLAW I REALLY HELPED HER WITH HER KIDS AND SHE GAVE ME HER BEHIND TO KISS. SUMMER SHE HELPED WHEN I NEEDED HER TO TAKE ME TO MY CHIROPRATOR BUT EVERY-TIME I WAS WITH HER IT SEEMED LIKE I WAS SET BACK. I DON'T UNDERSTAND.

Look I'm sorry I did say that, I've always been thinking about you, I have never seen you that way everyone has always looked up to you, and now you were asking me to help you. Said Zina.

A YO CHIEF I STARTED ALL OVER AGAIN I KNEW NOTHING I WAS ILLIERATE PEOPLE TOLD ME I LOOK LIKE A CARCK HEAD, EVEN THOUGH THEY SAW ME GO THROUGH THINGS SO TRUMATIC. I DON'T GET IT!

Look what do you mean when you say flaw is acting funny?

THAT CHICK HAS GIVEN ME THE COLD SHOULDER, WHEN I ASKED HER WHAT HAPPENED SHE NOW DON'T WANT TO TELL ME NOTHING. I ASKED HER SHE JUMP STUPID. I HELPED HER WHEN SHE HAD NOTHING, I COULD HAVE GONE TO COLLEGE IN TWO THOUSAND FOUR. BUT I DESIDED THAT I WOULD NOT GO BECAUSE I DID NOT WANT HER TO DROP OUT OF SCHOOL. MAN I TAKE THAT BACK I SHOULD HAVE NEVER HELPED HER OUT WITH HER KIDS. EVEN THOUGH THEY ARE MY NIESE AND NEPHEW, A YO MAN I'M JUST LOOKING FORWARD.

WHAT DID SUMMER DO? Said Zina.

45

IT'S JUST EVERYTIME I FEEL HEALED FEELING A LITLE MORE BETTER THAN BEFORE, AND THAN I GET AROUND HER I DON'T KNOW WHAT IT IS I FEEL WORST. I FEEL SHE COULD BE WORKING WITH THEM PEOPLE, I DON'TK NOW I JUST FEEL THAT WAY. OVER ALL THINGS SHOULD NOT HAVE GONE DOWN THE WAY IT DID, IT WAS A SET UP.

I REMEMEBER THERE WERE CHICKS IN THE BAR WISPHERING AND STARRING AT ME AS IF THEY HAD KNOWN ME. THE GUY THAT I BECAME COOL WITH CAME AND ASKED ME IF I COULD FIGHT AND SOME GIRLS WERE HATING ON ME. WHAT'S UP WITH THAT?

YO, LET ME CALM DOWN A LITTLE.

(I)ShTruth Poetry takes a deep breath and calms down a little bit trying to brace herself.

I'M STRESSING THAT TO YOU! I DID NOT KNOW THEM, MY PROOF IS WHEN THE PEOPLE SAID MY NAME TO THE DOCTORS IT WAS SOME THING TOTALLY DIFFERENT, EVERTHING IS JUST NOW COMEING BACK TO ME I WAS SO DELAYED IN EVERYTHING. THEY SAID THE CAR WAS I JACKED AND I WAS BEATEN WITH A BAT. OVERALL THEY LIED!

THEY ARE LIARS!

THEY WERE OUT FOR THEMSELVES.

I never thought you would be the same. You seem strong. It seems like you have matured a lot. Said Zina.

The thing about it is I been drawing nigh to God asking him what happened, I have not had much sleep at night I always toss and turn I even wake up screaming and crying, at times when I awake I have tears streaming down my face, it gives me nightmares. I hate it! I hate it! When are things going to completely get better? I question myself and Jesus all the time. And the only thing that comes to my mind is serve him, with all my soul mind and strength. I DON'T CARE WHAT NOBODY SAY JESUS IS THE SAVIOR OF THIS

WORLD! They don't even know, what I know. I always hear the saints in the church saying Jesus is a true and living God and it is so true. As being brought up in the church I said I believe that, but I never searched the scriptures. Now that I have devoted myself to Jesus I realize it is so true, YES NOW I CAN TRULY SAY, JESUS IS REAL!

Yes ShTruth Poetry I see a great change in you, but knowing how you use to be things seriously changed. I remember when we use to sit on the porch and we use to play church and use always wanted to be a preacher. You and my cousin and we use to imitate the people in the church, it was so fun we really had a good childhood. Said Zina.

Yeah I know. One thing I have learned is that when I was a child, I should have stayed in a child's place. Said Neosha.

Definitely and I us to always tell you not to go and you would leave me. I use to cry and pray that God would protect you. I remember when you got with that older guy that was the biggest mistake you have ever made, he really took advantage of you. Said Zina.

I remember when he would tell me he was going to see his daughter and I use to sit outside in the car for hours. You have to be careful messing with them older guys they are manipulative. Their game is higher than yours, everything is for certain people but for you I recommend that you don't even do it. If he is older he should at least be four to five years older and that's it.

He ought to have felt dumb. That guy messed over you than he had nerve to tell you he had a four month old daughter! Said Zina.

You know what he told me that he had five kids and one was my age. He also gave me their names even till this day I believe it. Said Neosha.

So do you ever plan to be with someone again?

Nah man I'm chilling the bible said that a women that is without a husband is suppose to work on pleasing the Lord, than when she has a husband she is suppose to please her husband and the Lord. But I don't plan to be with a man, I'm planning to live by myself, and do whatever it takes to please Jesus. I find more peace and safety in him than I feel with anything in this world.

Well' what about children?

Forget it I won't have any; I just told you I plan to be by myself.

Zina starts crying.

Having a husband and children is what you always wanted; I can't believe you allow this to change you.

I have something to confess I fear commitment, I fear love, I fear everything. I'm just walking by faith. The bible say there is no fear in love and you must have love in your heart to please God. But he is gonna have to help me with this. I don't know.

Zina cries harder.

What is you crying for?

I miss my Neosha.

Man please don't anybody care about me!

I do that's why I called I don't care no matter what you go through from this point on I'm gonna stay by your side.

Neosha started crying very hard; no matter how hard she tried she could not repress her tears.

I can't believe it. I can't believe it, glory hallelujah thank you Jesus.

I love you. Said Zina.

Thank you. Said Neosha I cannot believe it.

Neosha sat in the bathroom on the toilet seat she could not stand up anymore her knees started to buckle.

I don't know what to say I got to see this. I got to see this. Said Zina.

I even applied for the military.

but I knew deep down in my heart the state of being I was in I would not be able to get in, I would have cracked under pressure, when I went there my bones were still broke. I was not as strong minded as I was, back in two thousand and four. Because I applied then because my uncle wanted me to leave where I was staying, he did not want me to finish school and get knocked up, he said the opportunity is out there go get it. It even shocked him that I graduated so young. I was only doing it for him, but the thing about it was I was only doing it for him. He said go out explore see what else is out there, write your books get it published, don't let nobody stop you now. Than after the car accident while I was bed stricken he said all man her life is ruin I tried to get her to get away before anything could happen, now she' s gonna have to have somebody spoon feed her she can't do nothing.

Neosha began to break down Zina could hear it in her voice.

Look if you don't want to talk about you don't have to. Said Zina.

Neosha started to sniffle, trying to cough her breath.

I should have listened. I tried only thing about time you can't tell nothing and you have to finish your term. Even after it's over everything has to remain confidential or you will be thrown in a high prison.

I just went up there showing effort that I tried to do something besides my bones at the time was broke and you cannot go into the service if you had a history of broken bones.

I did not know that.

That's one thing they ask you.

The Sargent told me I was smart and if this did not work out for me, I should become a doctor because I have a high I.Q. He just kept telling his buddy I was smart and he said I could see it. I told them my situation, 'cause they saw the way I walked, and how I was delayed in speech so they asked what brings me there? And all I could do was cry, I said I don't want to be nothing I am trying my best and nobody can see. I was in a car accident and I was thrown out head first and on to big rocks by the railroad tracks and it broke my bones, I began to hyperventilate and they told me to relax. It took a while then I came to grips. I showed them the bruises on my arm and said this is what is did to me. I only want to please my uncle I want to show him I can do it.

Than the other Sargent asked me what I fear I said not pleasing God and going to hell, and being poor, I refuse to be a beggar. Than they looked at each other. The Sargent said what hurts the most I said nothing really it just that I could feel the pulse behind my ribs and my ribs are fractured so when I move I can feel it rubbing against my lungs. One of them asked do you plan on writing a book or doing a movie? I said I would I never thought about it. All they could say is that I was strong.

God is my witness.

No I believe you wow that's amazing. That's good so you feel getting away from here is what you need. Asked Zina.

Certainly.

How are you going to do that?

I'm starting college on January third this year two-thousand-seven.

Zina could not form her words, she paused for a long three minutes than she cried hard.

Neosha you're going to school? I cannot believe it you step it up big time! You just could not read, write or think for yourself, than you went to the military while your bones were fractured. You went to the high places to get started, now your started school. I want to believe in Jesus like you believe!

Noesha began to praise the Lord.

Hallelujah thank you Jesus

Thank you Jesus! I COULD NOT DO THIS WITH OUT YOU! YOUR MIGHTY YOU ARE THE EXDOUS, ALL POWER IS IN YOUR HANDS WITHOUT YOU I WOULD BE DEAD SLEEPING IN MY GRAVE YOU GAVE ME JOY TODAY AND HOPE FOR TOMORROW!

THANK YOU JESUS! Said Noesha.

Yes! Yes! Yes! Thank you Jesus! I believe in you Jesus thank you for helping my friend! Thank you Jesus hallelujah! Rejoiced Zina.

I don't know I will see how long this friendship would last, because I believe that one day you would go to. I feel God is trying to move all the old time people (friends and family) out of my life. So that he could start something new in my life. Said Neosha.

No I'm going nowhere I will prove to you that I am here to stay. Said Zina.

Class started January

Professor Blues stood in front of the class taking attendance. Holding a pencil in his hand marking names. Then he looked around announcing names.

Professor Blues
Jenifer.

Jenifer
Here.

Professor Blues
Paris.

Paris
Present!

Professor Blues

Luke.

Professor Blues

Neosha.

Neosha

Hi, how are you doing praise the Lord! God is good.

Professor Blues

Yeah. Um uh praise him.

Shaking his head trying not to smile.

Everybody

Laugh.

Professor Blues

John.

John
laughing very hard.

Hello present.

Professor Blues
Yeah. You (focusing on Noesha)

Neosha
How art thou doing?

Professor Blue
Hu.
Professor Laughs.

What are you?

Neosha
I'm Christian I believe in Jesus Christ!

John
Don't all Christian believe in Jesus?

Neosha
No some believe in the mother Mary.

John
Yeah that's him mother.

Neosha
Yeah but I believe in the son, Jesus pray to, I do salute her but I do
not worship her.

Everybody
stares at Neosha, than gradually they ask her questions.

Luke
A yo man I don't believe in god, I am a atheist.

Neosha
Yeah. But a fool says in his heart there is no God.

Luke
Luke gets a little bothered by her words.

It's a free county I can believe what I want to believe.
Neosha
Never said you couldn't but Jesus is the God that I serve.
And he is a true and living God.

Professor Blues
Okay guys please.

Moving his hands up and down saying

Easy. Easy.

Professor Blues closes his attendance book.

Okay look everybody this is college I will not ask you if you have your homework if you do not bring it in I will just mark a zero in my book. You are responsible for yourself I do not call parents, if you do not understand something ask questions. I believe that if a my kid went to school, come home and can't do his work by himself the teacher did not do his or her job. Here I do my job my biggest thing is ask questions if you do not understand something ask. There is nothing wrong with asking. It is vital to come on time. Do everybody have their books?

Professor Blues look around at the desks.

        Professor Blues
Please bring your books in next class.

I yelp I will truly appreciate it so that we can get started.
Before you know it, it will be May. So please bring your
books and be on time for class. Yelp you can go now
        class is dismissed.

Neosha slowly packs her bag and Professor Blues
began to talk to the some of the students after class.

A MONTHS LATER

Neosha sitting at her desk fighting the imagery in her head. Tears
streams down her eyes, turning her head side to side, holding her
mouth shut tight trying not to scream.

        Professor Blues
What's wrong? What's the matter?

        Neosha
Nothing.

Neosha is trying not to calm what's going on.

        Professor Blue
Look if you want to talk about it we can.
Right guys.

        Everybody
Yeah. Yeah. Lets talk. Don't hold it in what's bothering you?

Neosha

Look can I please call Jesus name to myself low.

Luke

Yeah go ahead.

But why do you have to do that?

Neosha

I am Pentecostal of the Apostolic Faith and we call on Jesus to keep our minds on him when, we are tarry meaning waiting on Jesus to fill us with the Holy Ghost, the name of Jesus has power to cast out any spirit.

Luke

Yeah what spirit?

Neosha

Any unclean spirit.

Professor Blues

I see you look a little better since you have called on your God.

Everybody

Yeah. That's true.

Neosha

I just keep seeing the car accident I was in.

Jenifer

what car accident? Was it bad?

Neosha takes a deep swallow

Neosha

Yeah. I still can't believe it, it should not have gone

down like that. I don't care what nobody has to say
it shouldn't have.

Professor
well tell me what else is going on in your mind.

Paris
it seems like it's something bigger.

Neosha
what I'm thinking maybe a little inappropriate
for school.

Professor Blues
This is college I am not going to call home.

Neosha
I had a vision of what is to come. Jesus showed
me how it will be in the last a terrible and great day.
When he comes back and crack the sky and all the souls
that are going to try to get saved and can't. Get saved meaning
being filled with the gift of the Holy Ghost.

Jenifer
That sounds wearied. The Holy Ghost.

Paris
Its a Christian thing, I'm Christian to.

Jenifer
So only Christians can get it, how much do it cost, it sounds
expensive?

Neosha
Look you cannot pay for it is free the spirit of Jesus comes on the
inside. It is a quickening spirit; it's something that is going to rise us
up in the last day when the angle blow the trumpet.

My word to everyone is get the Holy Ghost while you can because when Jesus return it will be too late. You may have your worries and cares now, but Jesus is going to take us to Heaven where there is everlasting life. Where we don't have to work no more, no more tears, no more pain, no more suffering, we will then live in perfect peace. We will have our own mansion and we will walk the streetsof gold.

All that Jesus revealed to Neosha she told the class. One thing Jenifer believed in was in incarnation, She was Hindu Neosha told her that Christians believe in the incarnation. The bible speaks of those that shall rise in that last day shall be changed in a twinkling of an eye. And we shall then be immortal we will not see corruption. The dead are gonna rise first then the living only the saints. Class ended in May Neosha was mugged the day before the final class in Newark after she had finished shopping for her niece and herself. She had gotten her hair done by some females. One said yes so they went into the pool hall her name was (Fly) her niece was sitting in her stroller. She was only two years old (FLY) best friend played with her while Neosha was getting her hair done. Neosha had no pockets so she put her money into her shopping bag. While (FLY) was talking to Neosha, the best friend said can we see what you got. Neosha forgetting that her money was in one of the bags said yeah. And got robbed. (FLY) told her she was done and that she had to go. Neosha cleaned the floor and pulled out a ticket she purchase before she got on the train. And left. She made it home safely but the next day she realized she had been robbed.

The folks in the class wanted to learn more about the Pentecostal Apostolic faith belief. But because that occurred it set her back to the belief she had. "That it is a cruel and mean world were living in. And people can be cruel"

Professor Blues said he believe her story and would help her on her movie. Proceeding that if she needed any advice about how to do anything she could email him on the campus emailing address.

Professor Blues and the rest of the class was enthuse on how Neosha matured so much from what she had went through, and still had the ambition to attend college, the thing that is so challenging, and chose one of the most technical major (radiology). Professor Blues one time insisted that it may be best for her to take a break for a while then come back. But having a fear so insist the she would become poor, she insist that she should go on. Many asked for her opinions in class and was highly admired. Professor Blues admired her intentions so much the he recommended that she be the director of his movie. And he wanted the women to take on the form of modesty she had, which was wearing long shirts, and Long and quarter sleeves. The only thing that stole from the drive she had was being mugged, so she turned down the offer and told him if there is something you want to do, do it. "No matter what they say, no matter how hard it gets, do it! Let no one steal your goals or your dreams. We are in America were you can dream so dream, making sure you bring it all the fruition. JESUS LOVES YOU SEEK HIM WHILE YOU CAN."

"To all thank you and my philosophy that we met to exhort one another, and believe that God will carry you through that trial and tribulation and bring you out, to share with others the goodness of Jesus Christ in the land of the living 'cause when it's night no man worketh."

To everyone "don't let it be said too late. Too late to enter in at the golden gates."
"Be not only a dreamer but live out your dreams!"
Truly with all my heart I love to say THANKYOU!
THANKYOU JESUS!

★ ★ ★ ★ ★ ★ ★ ★ ★

Unforgettable Quotes

Reading Class

"You know why don't you just quite." Said Professor Blues.

"No because I know that this a away to help me grow and become independent. One thing I have learned in the twenty years I've been living, is that you should never have to depend so much on a person, to where if they fall, I fall with them. My greatest fall is depending on a man that will never change, making the wrong friends, and defining people that would not define me." Said Neosha.

"I know you have a lot of people you have to prove yourself to, what would you tell them when you see them again, and you have graduated and have done your movie." Professor Blues.

"I would say what do you want now? Why are you all in my face? I remember you always called me poor. And said I will never be nothing. Why insist on wasting my time, we don't ever have to speak again. "Said Neosha

"You know what class." Said Neosha

(Everybody said)" What."

"These were the same characters that fought me and said I have nothing, and that I need to change. I always looked at them and said who are? I have never seen you before in my whole entire life. Get out my face. Overall little did they know I was graduating high school at the age seventeen and I feel I looked more prettier then, but in my eyes they were envious."

Everybody Said. "Yeah they were stay away from them."

Math Class

Everybody was introducing themselves to the class. By saying their names, their major and why they chose to go to college.

Everyone went and it was Neosha's turn.

"Yeah. What I have to say is that my name is Neosha my major is radiography and I chose to attend college so that I could get away from the people that kill dreams. Have no ambition always putting me down like they are better than me. I am courageous and know I can do this matter of fact this is the best decision I have ever made in my entire life because high school was the worst. And no matter what I go through Jesus will always be with me. That is why I chose to attend college." Said Neosha.

Everyone gaze with their mouth open.

"Aunty Neosha, you are so smart don't let nobody tell you, you are dumb. I seen you go through the most hardest things in life and you are better off then I seen many that have never been through the things you have gone through." Nephew 1

"If they tell you you're stupid laugh at them." Nephew 2

"I don't know why you're starting college
you aint gonna graduate."

"Watch people, where ever they could stop you they will." Neosha.

"One thing I have learned is that when Jesus is trying to tell you something I need to wake up and heed." Said Neosha.

"I hope you learn to choose your friends, more wisely." Doctor.

"You got to take him at his word" Pastor Ivory.

"Be for real! Be for real! Holiness is to be
perfected, be serious." Bishop.

Jesus moved and you weren't ready. "Reggae Artist

"It was God." Reggae Artist

Don't sue so quick, you got to let the case grow." Anonymous

Write a book. Who cares what they say. Young sister. So what
who cares what they say let them believe what they want to
believe. It's your life you got to live it, write a book I want
to read it. I believe your Father in Heaven will be proud. I'll
be honest I believe in you. I look up to you be strong your
strong. Tell your story. Let them fight you. You can fight.
You went through that so God can use you. Look at me,
I'm poor, I got nothing I come in here so I can eat and have
shelter. So what who cares. So what let them believe what they
want to believe. The only way you will let them get away is
if you do not write the book. That's what the judge said.

Neosha's response.

I believe you are at the state of redemption, only because you
lived on the streets, and you are looking for shelter. That is a
sign of being uncomfortable. When you break the net is when
you began to build something new. You need to write a book
also, go to church I am Pentecostal. There are all kinds of people
with all kinds of issues they testify about how Jesus delivered
them. You need to hear other people testimony that maybe
for you. and you will learn also to that you can overcome.

I call it watching Jesus.

Do good only you can make the change.
Just believe God will be with you.

His response

I know Pentecostal what denomination of Pentecostal are you

Neosha response

"I am Apostolic"

His response

"I'm going to be Apostolic"

"I'm changed said the man."

While in rehab Neosha was speaking to a man she
believe was gifted, but he sees himself as poor.

"They left me for dead and said they were trying to help. If they were trying to help me, in- stead of calling his friend who lived three minutes away, they would have called the cops. They lied I did not know what was going on, people always need something to say." Neosha.

"Who in the heck go through a car accident, come home, can't read and say I want to go to college. A yo that junk cracked me up when she said she wanted to start school." Sisters talking.

Neosha begged her sister to put her in school, and the whole time her sister was getting things ready Neosha played along. When her sister finished and everything went through she said. "I can't even read, or hold a pencil but I am going to learn how to do it, I don't care." And her sister said. A Sapphire if I had known that I would not have done that for you." Sapphire said. You never know how much you are helping a person when you show them that they can get ahead. Thank You." Her sister was heated. ShTruth Poetry laughs. Her sister thought about it longer and said "yeah that's true."

JESUS WAS THERE!

When my so called friend and friends left
me for dead. Jesus was there.

When I had no way to turn. Jesus was there.

When I lost all hope, and seen no way. Jesus was there.

When I didn't know who to call friend. Jesus was there.

All I know is Jesus. He is the truth, my guiding star. Jesus.

When I didn't know me. Jesus taught me.

When I almost lost my mind. Jesus saved me.

When my so called friends betrayed me. Jesus was there.

When I endured all the verbal abuse.
Jesus was there and said not so.

When I wanted God to multiply me talents Jesus gave unto me.

Jesus words saved me.

When I was down in dismayed All I know was. Jesus was there.

When I was sick and thought it was the
end of my world. Jesus spared me.

When I asked for forgiveness. Jesus had mercy on me.

Whenever I needed healing. Jesus send down his healing power.

Threw it all Jesus saved me and guide me
in the path he wanted me to go.

Jesus is my salvation and the light unto my path.

Jesus he'll be with us until the end of the world.

DISTANT LAND

Mommy I miss u
but this time I'm gonna have to let u go
I didn't send a letter to dis u
but you are remote
I laugh to shadow my tears
they see no tears
they R there
broken hearted is what they call me
I have to move on
so that I can grow
when Jesus come back
I plan to be with u
I didn't send this letter to dis u
I can recall the things you've taught me
like don't play with them boys
you are a girl
little ladies keep their skirts down
don't let nobody play with your kitty cat
stuff like that
other were too hard to mention
the last time I seen you
you was in a coffin
my words u couldn't hear
my tears you couldn't see
my yell was distance
I wished that u were here
so much until you became a nightmare
and I hated u
I guess I made the wrong prayer
I said Jesus send my mother back to me
I don't care how u do it!
by the grace of God I over came

but I didn't send this letter to dis u
I just have to let go
Mommy you are so; remote
the feelings make me choke
can anybody hear? NO
without u I couldn't breathe
(the time of my car accident code blue)
until God gave me oxygen
I turned my life over to Jesus
I did what you dreamed of
I wish u were here
not like that
I mean when I meet you in the air
before I go
I didn't send this letter to dis u
but you are remote
this time I'm gonna have to let u go
Lord knows I miss u

PO'EMS

WHO

My body aches I can barley move
I'm screaming for help
Inside, no one hears,
Who come when I call for help
Who's there to comfort my confused
Tears, who's there?
Who'll answer my cry?

Which way to turn
Lord please hear my call
I plead, I don't know why I'm dealt
This hand, but I am.
You say you love me,
You confuse me
On how you test my faith
Which way do I turn
You'll never leave you say
You'll never abandon me I believe
This I don't understand
Which way to turn

O happy day
You healed my pain
You asked for a little faith,
I gave, and I received
A blessing no man can take,
It was all faith.

Scales

Blind scales removed
Reviled a lot that help my case
You revealed things people tried to grave
I can't ask for no more than what you've given me
Thank you now I see

Smile

Hidden behind a smile
Pain, grief, fear, shame
No understanding
What's hidden behind a smile
Um, funny
I can't see the reason, to
So why do?
No what's really hidden
Behind is tears

Tears of Pain
I laugh to shadow my tear
For no man to see,
Bright teeth a happy face
No, all it is, is tears
Memories of history
Tore in to pieces
But all you see is a smile
To shadow my tears
My smile my tears
My smile my laugh
My tears
Not of joy
But all you see is a so called
Smile but it's really tears

Head Ace

Leave me alone
Stop asking me questions
I don't remember
Please stop asking me
I have no answer
I barley know my name
You assume everything is mendacious
So please stop asking me questions

Excuse me

O I remember
I forgot, O what happened it's my thoughts
Brain storming, mind slowly drifting
Imagination running away with me
Buzzard thoughts, not my character
What's going on, am I going crazy
Lord Please Save Me!
No these are not my ways
Neither my thoughts
I'm slowly going
Drifting from reality
O I remember, I forgot, O what happened......

Thank you

Thank you, I love you
Thank you, for helping me
Thank you for encouraging words
Praying I make it through
Thank you

You

it was you that carried me
Man was about to kill me
Hell, I visualized,
I'm a witness
Life you are, life you give
Mercy in your name
I have no shame
It wasn't I, it wasn't them,
It was you that carried me!

Said

You said not to tell
You said not to tell
I wish I knew
I wish I was smarter
I couldn't think
You manipulated me
I believed everything
All alone I you set me up for failure
You had me set my self up
Thought you was my friends

I can't snap out of this
What's going on?
Jesus please remove this from me
I don't want to suffer any more

The sun is shinning at the end of he tunnel
Life is what I give,
Life is in me,
This is who I am,
That is what I was,
Today you make plans
Tomorrow is your destiny
There's nothing you cannot do.
"Keep faith everything will fall in place."

I'm so happy I didn't give up,
I'm glad to say Jesus has blessed me
With talent no man can take!

Summer Madness

Darn all of this affliction, so abstruse
to handle no none comprehend my struggle
all appears to them is trouble.

Every day I arise and thank God
but then I ask myself why?
I attend church, give him praise
sometimes i'll pray, and wait for God's reply
a lot of foul thoughts cross my mind

summer madness June 18th 2005
independent no longer
nugatory I felt
so stiff no sleep
only prayer could help

Addiction

May

I can't let go he needs me, no he need God he has an
addiction I pray someday he'll surrender before it gets too bad
I pray every night asking the Lord to bless because he's slowly dieing

Physically you can see a slight
change in his features
I love him it's not all about the money, I just want him to see the light

deep down inside something is telling me to
go astray he must change
on his own but I refuse to allow him to damage himself
what make me makes me
clang longer is when they say
"never give up no one"

I can predict the brighter day

Lord I put it in your hands
i no longer know what to do

Untitled

don't be like no one
be yourself
you don't need no man to keep
you happy
stay in church
thank you for keeping your faith in me

everybody move at their own paste
don't listen to the negative
take heed to the positive things
remain in church

you have only one life to live
when you choose, choose right

all the positive things some said
keep me striving for what I believe

don't compare yourself to no one
start your own path and leave a trail

I SAID

Some said

March

Your strong your beautiful
you have a long life ahead of you
don't give up

thank you for encouraging me when my head was hung down

look down the street what do you see?
LTHERE'S A BIG WORLD OUT THERE EXPLORE

go to school
don't be like others
your smart your intelligent
God has something for you

Keep your head up
Only God Can Judge You

I dig your style
your different from the rest
you are the ruler of your destiny
"lively up yourself"
don't live on your past for you can't change

all the positive things some said
keep me going each day

you should model
you have a nice figure
you're going to be somebody
your thoughtful

MEANINGS

Life is hard you run into a lot of dead ends, life is not easy
tomorrow is not promised,

Today is present, yesterday is the past,
tomorrow future, dreams make it last,
dreams is plan, succeeding is an others,
dreams can be helpless if you don't
follow up on it, trying is the beginning,

searching is a start, outside is nature,
seasons change so do you,
one minuet it's light next it's dark,

that's the way of life,
mistakes you learn from obstacles come and go;

friends come and go so does men,
heartaches

and pain emotions, waterfalls don't chase
if not meant to be let it go, forgive or forget,
it's up to you;

conflicts the way of life,
decisions is up to you, your actions your accountable for,

business take care of, love yourself you came first – respect also,
time;
time is not on tout side one thing you can't
stop
even if you wanted to – giving up is a option,

trees grow fruit so do we,
when you first begin you start off with the blue print
step two
foundation after that you build upon that's

the same with knowledge
you don't walk before you crawl before you walk
that's the way it starts;

"where there's a beginning there's an end"
"I'm going to continue on with this pin
I'M OUT REMEMBER MY MEANINGS."

"NEVER THE LESS MY QUOTES"

poetry

Alone

Alone is where solitude lies
Solitude in my room
Just listening to myself
Getting peace of mind
Out of all I've been through
Alone
Alone
Just waiting for the reply of the most high
Alone
With the goal of finding souls
Speaking peace in the mist of the storm
Alone
Gravitating thoughts
Of being freed with Jesus
In peace
On earth
When all meekness, shall occur
Just looking all around I'm glad to see
How much I'm blessed

"Sometimes when I'm standin'
It seems like I done walked for miles

And my heart could be cryin'
Dead in the middle of a smile"
The Storm Is Over Now" R Kelly

Neosha was sitting in class when she was in a day dream. In the day dream R Kelly came up to her and said. "Stop crying, baby girl the storm is over. Look at what you have come from and thank God. Stop crying Jesus is good, there is no telling what you will have to go through, but realize Jesus called you.

Stop crying baby girl the storm is over now;

"I'm a prisoner
Of words unsaid
Just lonely feelings
Locked away in my head" **P.O.W ~Alicia Keys**

Neosha use to be condemned all the time about what she should have done. And she read Alicia Keys book and began to cry and ponder on the words saying to herself. "Yeah ya'll can say what ya'll want. None of ya'll been through this; I suffer all night and day tossing and turning, waking up screaming internally; yeah only if ya'll knew. She never knew the words to say to express herself; they just didn't know.

"Christmas you weren't with me
New Year's Eve you were not around
Valentine's came and went
Makes me wonder where your time was spent" No Happy Holidays
Mary J Blige

Neosha had just walked in her lover's house after a long day. Singing this song and her boyfriend saw her pasting back and forth as if she was sending a message to him. He got up and began to hit her demanding that she is never going to sing a song like that in his house again.

"Now if you listen closely
I'll tell you what I know
Storm clouds are gathering
The wind is gonna blow." *ALONE* **Maya Angeluo**

This poem means a lot to me because; no one on earth can live in
solitude. And just when I when I say I'm all alone, I look around
and realize there is someone that is going ough through some
of the same issues I'm facing. In life I feel some people are so
Cold hearted and no one truly understands.
But at times when I tell what I've been
through, no matter the race, belief or
Religion I realize no one on earth can't make it out here alone.

* * * * * * * * *

Grasping understanding of what they say is true.

Leaving me all discombobulated,

This all seems unreal to me.

Coming out of my character acting a fool.

What am I to do?

I pray this will all fade away real soon!
They said that it will surcease
I just have to follow guidelines.

When I think about my issues it make me want to cry.

An ask why?

Nah I must transform the negative
Energy to positive

Yes I can escape misery and cry no more.
I ask myself how can I talk to my
Family and not think about what I've done
No need to blame, myself for my

Past mistakes,
But it's abashing
All I can do is pray that Jesus
Can relieve me from my afflicted mind.
Yes He Will

Think

They believe my side of the story partially
only because of my mentality
saying things occurred when they had–en
crying making them believe only made them madder
when they.....
refusing me, but listening to the enemy
something sound strange
how are they gonna listen to the one's that, tried to killed me
but God set me free
made up a cover story, to avoid actuality
saying I had been beaten
when it was a car accident
ain't that strange

think

believing what old time friends say when they weren't even there

think

how are you helping me
wrongfully accusing the innocent

think

how are we gonna let them get away from this

think

who's side are you really on?

Think?

We Ani't Friends

I see you married
Good for you
Many blessing be with you
Marriage is beautiful
It's what God approve of
Messed up how you did it
Creped with the enemy
To find some loving
Something how there's people on your side
To many you looking right
Not in my eyes
Good for you
I'm glad not to be at or in your wedding
I hope you don't call me your friend
Friendship is not with you and me
I don't want to greet
You go your way, I'll go mine
Whispering to foes telling secrets
We aint friends
Have me misunderstood
Thought I would approve
I won't bring this up anymore to you
But I will remember, how you help let enemies flee'
All I have to say is good for you
Many blessing be with you

Silent Foes

my insides got me blind and I can't see
the words that people have embedded in me
silent enemies
speak with myths
words of my family I could not hear
silent foes got the best of me
best friends turned down hands to me
instead I smile
inside I die
committing suicide in my own mind
nobody can hear
so many sight
she's stupid she won't even speak
give me information so I can help you
listen closely here
because a crime has been committed
Sapphire please
listen to me instead I couldn't hear
the good Samaritans before me
they couldn't conquer me
the silent foes manipulated me
had me brain wash before you'll got to me
sorry family,
sorry Jesus, sorry me, me, self I didn't know
what was going on so I was
misstated and listened to silent foes
best friends turned their hands to me
now all is left is faithful family, true friends
above all Jesus, above all Jesus you spared me!
Wait a minute ya'll
I never got the chance
to express myself

I didn't forget I just couldn't recite
the tragedy occurred every time I thought
of the car flipping and being thrown
from the vehicle
Jesus had took me for seconds
to show me the other side whether life or death
death after death, life after life
it was my choice I chose life
Jesus is life
wait a minute in due season I will confess what happened
silent enemies creped up to me
and got the best of me (pause)

Stand

Soon as I find myself
And learn to keep my place
Not fall to my face
Not bow when they call me names
For they are wrong
They say most rumors are known to be true
I've known them to be myths
Soon as I find my self
And learn to keep my place
Not fall to my face
When they misjudge
When I dress in modest apparel
Perfecting godliness
In holy ways
They say they love Christ
And don't know his ways
I say their blind
And don't know him
They just call his name
They use it in prayers
Make believe
They pray for me, behind me,
Praying prayers to drown me
Who's ways are righteous
Falling and rising
Rising and falling
As soon as I can find myself
Learn more of myself
Soon as I find myself
And learn to keep my place
Not fall to my face
Bowing down to no one

Standing, where I stand
Perfecting holiness
Believing in God
Not man
Soon as I.
Soon as I find myself
Allowing no man on earth to deceive me
That they are the Christ
Soon as I find myself
Learning to keep my place
Not fallen to my face
Soon as I find my self
Learning to keep my place
Not fall to my face
Soon as I find my self

Robbed

They ask me how I feel
I keep all in, instead
I rather lie
But the truth comes out and robs me
Of all good
Sadness fills my mind
After all these years I still can't get a witness
I've been robbed
Of all I've owned
My sarcasm
My internal goal of jesting
I been robbed of my manners
The anger I really want to show
I've
I've been robbed
No knowing which way is forward
When people see they see a smile of one dying internal
Take it; it all will do you good
Happiness is longed for
Sadness is hidden
I rather go away to leave one blissful
Then to take one into the carriage I bare
I been robbed
Robbed
Robbed
Can't help but to keep all truths inside
While many lash out with words they refuse to hide
When I see one out spoken in some ways I praise them
Cause I rather" Speak my mind, and lose a friend. Then to keep a friend and hold all within."
I've been robbed
Of my motive to laugh out loud

Without one thinking
I'm too loud
I been robbed
Of forever knowing
I been robbed
Of feelings
Of feelings unbarring
I been robbed
People smile
But they have hidden unknowing
They say they are there for me
But they lie and say
All the best
They lie
They get away with lying
They are all lairs
They steal
My forever goings of goals
I'm robbed
Of all that I once was
I can now tell the truth in the real ones
And ask the others
Where is your kite?
Play with them, not me
Because I've been robbed
Of my first and last name
It's all showing
Robbed
Of blissfulness
All I do is put on fronts
With a kiss
Robbed
Of all truth
That I am happier without you

Robbed
Just robbed
Robbed
Robbed
Whosoever care let me know it!
They don't
It's true
I learned to thank God for me, and when I have truly letting go of
you, I learned to live. Out of all that's been taken. I learned to restore
with glue. True friends are hard to find.

Run Away

I figure if I could just run away
from everybody and start over again
things will change
all people remember is my hopeless dreams
I want to go here
I want to move there
I like this
I want that
is what everybody hear
so she dream......
hope-in they'll come to fruition
deep down in side she want's to run away....
run way..... from the pain
that has grown deep with in
the level of expression has now declined
try in to balance what's all in her mind
only if she could run away....
getting to the next state
will the past erase?
Hopefully
she can't stop bringing it up
when everybody keep saying
it's all your fault
you was in the wrong
should have been a bit wiser
and so on;
only if she could run away.....
escape the pain the anger,
the madness, the frustration
that has grown with in
just run away....
get away:
running to the next state

**Written in Ohio (riding through
on a missionary journey)**

My eyelids

Was the wiper for my eyes
My tears took away all the enduring fears
The power to move on is what
Was inclined in my heart

I will no longer get in Gods' way
Jesus is the God that I serve
I don't wish bad on none of them that default me
To gainsay
But from the point where I have forgiven truly
Those that crossed me and set snares in my path
For me to be confound
Has seem to have gotten over on me
But I don't give the devil any glory
Jesus allowed this obstacle for a purpose
It took years to over come
Many saw me down and laugh in my face
But I can truly say that I've been bless
Her I am to share
My testimony among mankind

Don't let your trials bring you down
Flip it and know
Deep down in your heart that Jesus is God and he loves you
Just because
Things were turned around realize things happen for a reason
No matter how much you try to fix the problem
Realize you can't
It over
Thank God it's done
Live for Jesus and he'll place genuine people in your life

He will not allow anyone to harm you
Be obedient
Follow his commandments
Turn from you wicked ways
Time draweth nigh when Jesus shall appear
Get the holy ghost (the spirit of Jesus in the inside)
Be true to yourself the pain can't stay

Vengeance I recompense sayeth the Lord

ShTruth Poetry found Jesus and is now a devout Christian

The names of the people are changed, the events are true

People look at Christians as denying they have scars, I have scars this is why I became more serious to God, because I know he is coming back and I know the miracles he performed in my life. I'm not ashamed of talking about Jesus Christ; all that I have comes from God.

Dear, Audience

I made the choice to share my life story because I had to learn the hard way not to run from God. I heard Jesus calling before the tragedy, I chose to not listen, and the price I paid was great. This book is a broad way of Jesus manifestation to me that he is real and if he allows something to happen it is for a reason. My question to you is do you hear him calling? Do you hear Jesus calling?

ShTruth Poetry

If you listen you will hear, you will see, you will know Jesus is calling. Why he's calling because he is coming back someday soon;

Printed in the United States
by Baker & Taylor Publisher Services